14

Antología del Sonoran

———————

Poems by
Christopher Bogart

A Publication of The Poetry Box®

©2018 Christopher Bogart
All rights reserved.

Editing & Book Design by Shawn Aveningo Sanders.
Original Cover Illustration by Robert R. Sanders.

No part of this book may be reproduced in any matter whatsoever without permission from the author, except in the case of brief quotations embodied in critical essays, reviews and articles.

ISBN: 978-1-948461-15-3
Printed in the United States of America.

Published by The Poetry Box®, 2018
Beaverton, Oregon
ThePoetryBox.com

For all who dare to dream the American Dream

Contents

Introduction	7
Nathum Landa Ortiz (Wellton 26/Survivor)	9
The Yuma 14:	
Edgar Adrian Martinez Colorado	10
Julian Ambros Malaga	11
Abraham Morales Hernandez	12
Arnulfo Baldilla Flores	13
Reyno Bartolo Hernandez	14
Efrain Gonzales Manzano	15
Heriberto Badilla Tapia	16
Lauro (John Doe #48)	17
Alejandro Maurin Claudio	18
Lorenzo Hernandez Ortiz	19
Enrique Landeros Garcia	20
Reymundo Barrerda Maruri Sr.	21
Reymundo Barreda Landa Jr.	22
Mario Castillo Fernandez	24
Reunion	26
Remains	27
Epilogue	29
Notes	30
Acknowledgments	31
Praise for *14: Antología del Sonoran*	33
About the Author	37
About The Poetry Box® Chapbook Prize	39

INTRODUCTION

"They were aliens before they ever crossed the line."
~ Luis Alberto Urrea, *The Devil's Highway*

In late May, 2001, twenty-six Mexican migrants were discovered in the Sonoran desert near Yuma, Arizona. Twelve of them were wandering around the desert, delirious and dying of thirst. As they were found, they were airlifted to the nearest medical facility. Fourteen were taken by pickup truck to the morgue. Together they are known as the Wellton 26. The deceased became known as the Yuma 14.

The oldest of the Yuma 14 was fifty-three and the father of the youngest, a fifteen-year-old boy. All fourteen were men. Most, even in their teens, were the sole support of their families. Many left behind wives and children. One or two were alone for most of their lives. All were alone in the morgue. The bodies of most of these men were claimed by their families. Only one of the bodies was never claimed. It was buried in a potter's field in Tuscon. He was known to the Wellton 26 only as Lauro. His grave marker reads: "John Doe #48."

Each of them was searching for his own American Dream. Instead of finding their dreams, they ended up dying in their own nightmares.

In researching each of these fourteen men, I relied heavily on Luis Alberto Urrea's book, *The Devil's Highway* as well as on the articles written at the time in the local newspapers. Under the names of each of these men, I have placed the map coordinates where they were found.

In the tradition of Edgar Lee Masters' *Spoon River Anthology*, I have let each of the members of the Yuma 14 tell his own story in the hope that their deaths, as well as their dreams, will not be forgotten.

Nathum Landa Ortiz

Wellton 26/Survivor

*There must have been thirty of us out there.
We were in trees to hide from the sun.
We were ripping open cactus.
We were drinking our own urine.*

*I could hear them out there screaming.
I saw them without water—
Out there. I saw them in despair.*

*Some died of desperation.
Some just lost their minds.
They fell out there—all alone.*

*I thought that I would die that morning.
The majority died that day,
I don't know how I survived.
Maybe it was a miracle.*

Edgar Adrian Martinez Colorado

Wellton 26/Yuma 14
(N. 32.21.85/W. 113.18.93)

I was born on the top of the Hill of the Eagle
In the province of Veracruz. Eight dollars a day
Was all I was worth to the Coca-Cola plant.

I played soccer on weekends, the star of my team
Till the day I met Claudia Reyes.
Eight dollars a day then
Just wasn't enough

So, at 16 years old, I walked to my death
In the desert in Arizona.

When I fell to the sand,
I heard eagle's cry,
The thump-thump-thump-thump
As it came down from the sky.
Too late to be saved.

      The sun seared my eyes—
      Sand sealed them closed,
      Burning . . . burning . . . .

Julian Ambros Malaga

Wellton 26/Yuma 14
(N. 32/W. 113)

I wore my favorite soccer shirt.
I carried nothing but a change of clothes,
A wad of dollars and pesos
A note from my new bride
A heart filled with promises
A head brimming with dreams.
I promised my mother a new house
With cement walls, a new stove.
I promised my uncle a reliable used pickup truck.
I promised my cousins I'd send for them soon.

I promised my father I'd behave with respect,
And that I'd always make him proud.

I was 25,
A veteran soldier,
A new husband,
An expectant father.

When I finally knew that I was truly lost—
I tore up my money.
I threw myself on burning sand,

My body was returned to my family in Chamizal.
I lie here now—in a field outside my hometown.

Soon my son will be 17.

Abraham Morales Hernandez

Wellton 26/Yuma 14
(N. 32.21.85/W. 113.18.94)

I had dressed for a race, not a marathon.
My black sweatpants were cooking me alive.
As we trod toward El Norte,
We eyed each other, wondering
Who would be the next one to fall.

Exhausted, I tripped and hit the dirt hard.
I crawled the dry ground rolling onto my side.
I kicked till I was under a bush.

The cries of the others
Faded in. Faded out.
Out was the last I remembered.

They spotted my tennis shoes,
Two small white will-o'-the-wisps
Peeking out from under the shrubs.

I took the long truck ride
As a man with no name.
I lay in a drawer,
As I had in the desert,
Waiting for someone to find me.

Desconocido.
Unknown.

Arnulfo Baldilla Flores

Wellton 26/Yuma 14
(N. 32.23.17/W. 113.19.45)

When *La Migra* finally found me,
I looked none the worse for wear;
My Converse sneakers, barely scuffed,
My white shirt—sharp contrast to my jet black hair

A wad of pesos stuffed in my pocket,
A folded letter never read.
I lie in the dust so peacefully,
It was hard to believe I was dead.

Reyno Bartolo Hernandez

Wellton 26/Yuma 14
(N. 32.23.16/W. 113.19.55)

So very peaceful here,
High on this hill
Overlooking fertile green fields
Of dark green leaves,
Bright red berries—
Arabica coffee beans.

It seems only yesterday
That I left San Pedro
In dark green pants and bright green sox
That my wife had bought for me
So that I would look good enough
To labor in America's fertile fields.

We adopted a four-year-old girl,
Augustina and I,
To give her a life
One we had never had.

She's 34 now.
I see her every day,
Working in those same green fields

For her
I wanted
So much more.

Efrain Gonzales Manzano

Wellton 26/Yuma 14
(N. 32.24.40/W .113.22.53)

We were born in the town of Villagrande,
Isadoro, Mario and Me.
There wasn't enough money in the family
To support one—much less three.

So we hiked our way through the Sonora
Hot sun beating down on our heads.
When I got too weak to continue,
They decided to leave me for dead.

Desperate, I crawled up the mountain
To see if I could find my way back
But *La Migra* finally found me, brought me back down,
Stuffed in a black body sack.

Heriberto Badilla Tapia

Wellton 26/Yuma 14
(N. 32/W. 113)

When I slipped past a dying saguaro
Needles stabbed my arms and my legs
I could barely feel their stings.

When I cracked my eyes open in the 'copter
I heard the thump, thump, thump of its blades
I thought that maybe I could be saved.

But when the medics stabbed my arm with the IV
I could not feel its sting.

It was too late
To feel anything.

LAURO (JOHN DOE #48)

Wellton 26/Yuma 14
(N. 32/W. 113)

I wasn't supposed to go on this trip
But Medrano never showed up
So Mendez asked me.

He was 19 years old. I was 29.

I should have known better
Than to listen to that *cabrón*
I should have known better.

The 14 travelers gave us $90
Sent us north for water.
We walked till we could walk no longer.

We had lit a dry bush so someone would find us,
Bright orange sparks floating up to the night sky.
Nobody came.

The last time I fell
I couldn't get up.
That 19-year-old *cabrón*
Pulled me under a bush.
I felt his sneaky fingers
Poking round in my pockets,
Searching for money—

Then I felt nothing at all.

I lie here now in a potter's field
Near Tucson, Arizona
Ageless.
Anonymous.

Alejandro Maurin Claudio

Wellton 26/Yuma 14
(N. 32.13.16/W. 113.19.51)

Wearing black pants
To trek through the desert
Was not the smartest of moves
But they really showed off
My green handkerchief,
And my silver belt buckle
With the head of a horse.

As we traveled through Mexico
I took out my mirror
To check out my outfit, my hair.

When we got to the desert
I walked in with Lauro,
Santillan and Berto Tapia.

When Javier babbled crazily,
We left him behind.

Lauro, Tapia and I never made it.
But Javier did.

Who's crazy now?

Lorenzo Hernandez Ortiz

Wellton 26/Yuma 14
(N. 32.23.18/W. 113.19.59)

My wife Juanita,
Our five kids in tow,
Rushed down the rock-strewn path
To the town's only phone
To hear the anonymous caller
Tell her
I was gone.

It was 110 degrees.
I ran out of water.

All I wanted was to rest.
I felt sick to my soul,
But I pushed onwards
Until I could push no longer.

I fell in the sand
Under an ancient saguaro.

When they finally found me
My stomach had caved in
Making my pants look empty.
Only my pelvis
Held up brown flesh
Like a tent
Coming loose
From its poles.

Enrique Landeros Garcia

Wellton 26/Yuma 14
(N. 32.23.17/W. 113.19.54)

It was a long long walk
From the coffee bushes of San Pedro
To the soybean fields of Illinois
But I was walking to a better life
For Octavia and Alexis, my son.

I loved my new dyed leather cowboy boots
But I had to leave them behind.
When Octavia saw them
She hugged them to her heart
And she cried.
She knew I had gone.

They found me in the desert
I was clothed in blue jockey shorts.
My teeth were all broken.
I had gnashed them violently in pain.
They no longer bother me now.

Now my son is seven
And helps Octavia tend the plants
In the coffee bean fields of San Pedro.

My long dead ears can still hear the fear
Of my young son's plaintive cry:
Please Daddy! Please! Please don't go!

Reymundo Barreda Maruri, Sr.

Wellton 26/Yuma 14
(N. 32.23.16/W. 113.19.52)

I was *mestizo* on my mother's side,
A hard worker all of my life,
Farming the land and bottling Coke
Until the factory laid me off.
I wanted my family to have so much more
Than a small house with the leaky roof.

My son was my pride,
My king of the world.
A high spirited fifteen year old,
I feared leaving him behind.
He finally convinced me
If we worked together,
We could earn enough money
To patch up the roof
To give him a room of his own.

By 2:00 pm, it was 108 degrees.
We had run out of water hours before,
And my little king was stumbling.
Andale, m'ijo! I coaxed him along.
"I'm coming, papa," he sighed.

He fell to the ground for the very last time.
I held him so tight,
Rocked him wrapped in my arms
Until he was gone.
I threw myself on the sand,
Suddenly so cold,
And swam till I could swim no more.

Reymundo Barreda Landa Jr.

Wellton 26/Yuma 14
(N. 32.23.19/W. 113.19.56)

I was my dad's pride and joy,
An honors student in my school,
The star of my home soccer team,

As the bus drove us north,
I sat in the front windshield,
My comic books in my lap.

I felt like I was
The king of the world—
Going to America.

I wore black pants
As we walked the Devil's Highway.
The woody plants tore my arms,
The heat of the sun
Cooked my legs
Like *salchichas* in their skins.

"Let's go, son." My father pulled me forward.
Ahí voy papa! I told him
In an effort to be brave.

But I was too sick to feel that brave.

Moaning ever so softly
I fell in the dirt.
I was burning inside—I was freezing outside.

Father held me in his arms.
His tears fell on my cheeks.

I am so alone on this cold metal gurney,
Swimming in black rubber space.
So very alone.

Mario Castillo Fernandez

Wellton 26/Yuma 14
(N. 32.23.16/W. 113.19.54)

I dropped out of high school
After my good looks
Bought me two children in two years.

By the spring of 2001,
I could no longer make enough money
To support my growing family.

I wanted furniture for the house,
A room for the kids,
New clothes for school
And *mochilas* to carry their books

I was a coffee and citrus worker
Maybe I could find work
In the orange groves of Florida
I loved oranges.
I wasn't afraid to work.

In time, I thought, we could open a bodega
Make tortillas for the lunch crowd.

I borrowed nineteen hundred dollars
Put my wallet in my blue jeans pocket
And polished my silver belt buckle,
With the fighting cock—

I was on my way.
I entered the desert on a hot May day,
110 degrees before noon.

Two days later,
My body was found.
I had not kept my good looks.

Reunion

Mendez abandoned us,
Deserted us to die.

We had not deserted each other.

We lined up head to toe
On stainless steel slabs,
Hugging the death house wall.

It was a short but silent reunion.
Even though our eyes were open,
We could see no more.

Listen! Can you hear the nitrogen gases?
They seem to sound like hopeless sighs,
Wandering aimlessly around our black body bags—
Their echoes piercing air for miles.

Remains

"They came to the broken place of the world, and taken all together, they did not have enough items to fill a carry-on bag."
~ Luis Alberto Urrea, *The Devil's Highway*

mesquite beans
green sox
one comb
one pair red underpants
one pair of jeans
one belt buckle with an inlaid fighting cock
one belt buckle with an inlaid spur
a pocket mirror
four Advil in a foil strip
Furor jeans
a piece of colored paper
two wallets (one brown)
a fake silver watch
six Mexican coins
a green handkerchief
a letter
Converse knockoff basketball shoes
Mexican bills
a blurred photo ID stained with sweat
fourteen deserted dreams

Epilogue

The Arizona Open GIS Initiative for Deceased Migrants documented 2,832 migrant deaths from 2001 through Aug. 10, 2017, using records from the Pima County Office of the Medical Examiner. The office conducts autopsies on remains found in the southern Arizona counties of Santa Cruz and Cochise, in addition to Pima. But migrants increasingly die crossing in other border states, including Texas, New Mexico and California. The Border Patrol tracks deceased migrants found by its agents but not those reported to other agencies. According to Border Patrol statistics, agents found 6,915 deceased migrants along the entire southwestern border from fiscal year 1998 through fiscal year 2016. The Tucson Sector was the deadliest, with a total of 3,654 deceased migrants found by Border Patrol agents over that period.

~ Daniel González,
"How many people die trying to cross the border?"
The Republic/azcentral.com, September 21, 2017

Notes

The poem, "Nathum Landa Ortiz," is a found poem. I have italicized the words in this poem because they are the survivor's own words, given in testimony after his rescue.

Some of the information, in regards to the exact location where each man was discovered, is unavailable at this time. Therefore, Julian Ambros Malaga, Heriberto Badilla Tapia, and Lauro (John Doe #48) are listed with approximate GPS coordinates: N. 32/W. 113, representing the general area in which all fourteen men were found.

The Spanish words and phrases used in these poems have also been italicized to identify them, and are defined below:

> *desconocido* = unknown
> *la migra* = immigration
> *cabrón* = bastard
> *mestizo* = half-blood, half-breed
> *andale m'ijo!* = Let's go, son!
> *salchichas* = sausages
> *Ahí voy papa!* = I'm coming, Papa!
> *mochillas* = backpacks

Acknowledgments

I owe a huge debt of gratitude to the meticulous research of Luis Aberto Urrea in the writing of his book, *The Devil's Highway*. It was his compassionate telling of the stories of the Wellton 26/Yuma 14 that inspired me to write these poems.

Information on the lives and deaths of the Yuma 14 also came from articles published in the *Tucson Citizen* and the *Tucson Republic*.

I would like to thank the members of Jersey Shore Poets, a group of poets in Monmouth County, NJ, for their support. Their critiques as well as their encouragement were crucial to the success this project.

Finally, I would like to thank the many hundreds of students who populated my classes over my teaching career, students who, with their families, had dared the perils of this journey to this country and whose hard work earned them a chance at an American Dream. The great majority of these young people were my hardest working students—cheerful, diligent and ever-grateful for their chance at a better life. Their hard work and determination were a source of inspiration to me and to their classmates. These poems, then, are for them as much as for the 14 migrants I have tried to memorialize, migrants who sadly were unable to take advantage of the chance to achieve their own dreams.

Praise for 14: Antología del Sonoran

"A cautionary tale written in dried blood, and a grim portrait of the consequences of impossible choices."

~ Gregg G. Brown, publisher, BLAST PRESS

"An informal and empathetic document as well as a poetic sequence, *14: Antología del Sonoran* elegizes and gives voice to those no longer able to speak their stories. Christopher Bogart's risky yet respectful poems honor the names of these dead, and insist that nothing can sever the bonds that connect us to each other."

~ Michael Waters, author of *The Dean of Discipline*

"The quiet calm of the poems in Christopher Bogart's *14: Antología del Sonoran* heightens the despair in the individual stories of these fourteen doomed men and lays bare the tragedy of lives lost in the simple yearning for human dignity."

~ Daniel Weeks, author
For Now: New & Collected Poems, 1979-2017

"'The U.S. - Mexican border *es una herida abierta* where the Third World grates against the first and bleeds,' Gloria Anzaldúa wrote in 1987. Three decades later, the open wound has grown deeper and wider, the need to address it and assist with the healing more urgent than ever. A poet citizen sharply aware of the power and limitation of art to bring about change, Christopher Bogart reminds us of the complicitous nature of silence. Soul-wrenching in the directness and sparseness with which they capture each voice, the poems of *14: Antología del Sonoran* speak of lives trapped in a system that makes dreaming for dignity a death sentence. Each poem performs a ritual that mourns, restores robbed dignity, and cries for justice."

~ Mihaela Moscaliuc, Associate Professor at Monmouth University
author of *Father Dirt* and *Immigrant Model*

"Christopher Bogart resurrects the 'Yuma 14' who died on the Devil's Highway that links Mexico to Arizona, seeking the kind of life most Americans take for granted. As their bodies lie in the burning desert or in the brilliant light of the morgue they tell us their stories, their dreams, their hopes. But this is not a book about hope. No, hope is not welcome here, just as these souls were not welcome in our country. 'For her I wanted so much more,' says one about his now fatherless daughter. 'It was hard to believe I was dead,' whispers another."

~ Peter E. Murphy, Founder
Murphy Writing of Stockton University

"The distant deaths of ordinary people usually don't make the news headlines and can be too easily ignored. In *14: Antología del Sonoran*, Christopher Bogart rescues 14 such deaths from obscurity and into compassionate focus, bringing their humanity to life. These were 14 men – among the unnumbered migrants – who risked everything to seek the American Dream of making better lives for themselves and their families. Bogart documents each man's death in poems that are both stark factual accounts and movingly eloquent portraits of individuals who dared to dream – and lost to the vast wasteland of the Sonoran Desert. Written with economy of language and vivid details, these poems bear witness to a daily human tragedy that, once you cross the border between knowing and not knowing, is unforgettable."

~ Linda Johnston Muhlhausen, author of *Elephant Mountain*

"Christopher Bogart sets his beautiful language against harsh, hellish landscapes, which mirror hardships faced by the men he writes about. Here is the hero's journey with little hope of transformation, or victory. These men accept the challenge despite the odds, and in these carefully crafted snapshots of their lives, Bogart shows us a terrifying sadness, beauty and bravery."

~ Deborah LaVeglia
(Moderator: "PoetsWednesday," The Barron Arts Center)

About the Author

Christopher Bogart is a retired educator and a working poet and writer with an MA in Creative Writing from Monmouth University. His poetry has been published in *Voices Rising from the Grove, Spindrift, WestWard Quarterly, Saggio Poetry Journal, The Monmouth Review* (2013, 2014), *Mind Murals* (2013), *Whirlwind Review* (Fall 2014), *The Howl of Sorrow,* a Collection of Poetry Inspired by Hurricane Sandy, *This Broken Shore* (Summer 2015, 2018) and *Jersey Shore Poets* (First Edition).

In 2015, he was chosen as First Runner Up for Monmouth University's inaugural The Joyce Carol Oates Award for Excellence in Fiction, Poetry, and Creative Non-Fiction. In 2017, he was chosen as one of two finalists for The Brian Turner Literary Prize for Fiction. He is presently writing poetry and short stories, translating the poetry of Federico Garcia Lorca and Arthur Rimbaud into English, as well as working on his first novel, tentatively titled *The Beast,* about two Central American teenage migrants who flee poverty and crime in search of a better life in America.

About The Poetry Box® Chapbook Prize

In 2018, The Poetry Box introduced their annual Chapbook Prize competition, awarding publication to at least one poet. The contest is open to both established poets and emerging talent alike, and the editors reserve the right to select more than one poet's manuscript for publication. Currently, the contest is open to poets residing in the United States and is open for submissions each year during the month of February.

2018 Winners

First Prize:
Shrinking Bones by Judy K. Mosher (New Mexico)

Second Prize:
November Quilt by Penelope Scambly Schott (Oregon)

Third Prize (tie):
14: Antología del Sonoran by Christopher Bogart (New Jersey)
Fireweed by Gudrun Bortman (California)

www.ingramcontent.com/pod-product-compliance
Lightning Source LLC
LaVergne TN
LVHW020457080526
838202LV00057B/6006